# Poetic Expressions

### Let the Children Show Us!

### By Judy Carol Dover

To order additional copies of this book, contact:
Xlibris
844-714-8691
www.Xlibris.com
Orders@Xlibris.com

ISBN:    Softcover            978-1-4257-0597-8
         EBook                978-1-6641-4492-7


Print information available on the last page

Rev. date:  11/24/2020

# Acknowledgments

First, I give thanks to my Lord and Savior Jesus Christ for the gifts and talents entrusted to me. In honor of my mother, the late Bennie Ida Sesley Dover—who greatly influenced my literary and musical abilities. To my instructors and professors at Limestone College for imparting your wisdom. To my instructors at Spartanburg Tech and the Arts Counsel for a certificate of excellence and blue ribbon in Celebrate the Arts 2004. I give heartfelt thanks to my friends and family, Edwards Printing Service Inc. (first draft), the Benjamin E. Mayes Alumni Association, the library staffs of Limestone College, and Cherokee County. And last but not the least, the Spartanburg County Foundation (two scholarships).

# Chapter 3
## Inspirational and Informative

Am I but a Tree?

From Africa to Riches

Gotta Climb Atop That Mountain

Let the Children Show Us

Life Is like a Ball Game

Silent Cry of a Victim

Street Moods

Sunshine after the Rain

Tragedy at Columbine High

Wisdom

Longing for the Night

## Short Stories

Laretha Sinclair Furgason

What the United States Flag Means to Me

Introduction to Children's Book

# Dedication

My children, grandchildren and family,
our youth of today and tomorrow, and also to my hometown—historical Cowpens
nestled—in the Upstate of South Carolina.

# And He Made Them Male and Female

## How different are we?

The old cliché—that men and women are extremely diverse in nature—is good cause for examination. First, we look at interrelated relationships among adolescents. Having grown up with five brothers, I soon noticed our diversity. My sister Myrtle and I chose to play with dolls, tea sets, or jackstones, while my brothers chose to pitch horseshoes, build wooden wagons, or shoot marbles. My older brothers assisted my father in the fields and worked weekends at the café before finding jobs that are more conducive. Their chores and duties were outside, but my older sister (Nellie) assisted mama in the house. The mere fact that our chores and hobbies were different indicated that we were also different. How different are we? My two middle brothers (Leon and Quinnon) would sometimes challenge my older sister (who, along with my oldest brother, was in charge when my parents were working) as she assigned them chores. Their defiance was related to their masculine pride, of course. Nevertheless, she would eventually coerce them into doing what she asked, even if she had to use "hickory tea." *Chuckle!* Hickory tea is the connotation of a hedge or tree branch used for spanking children. Quinnon and Leon seemed a little rambunctious with Nellie at times because she had to act in behalf of my parents. Nevertheless, my oldest brother (Nathan Jr.) could easily bring them under control. He was like our second dad— firm, straightforward, and persuasive. Yet he taught my three middle brothers to be responsible. Hubert, our second older brother (now deceased) seemed a little rebellious at times—prompting Nathan Jr. to discipline him. Contrariwise, Nellie didn't have any trouble instructing Myrtle and me. As younger siblings, we simply honored her as our oldest sister. Boys heeded the teachings of our parents, pastors, and scout leaders. As girls, we adhered to the teachings of our grandparents, other female family members, and teachers. Elderly neighbors and community youth leaders often took the time to teach and mentor us as well. Besides, guiding children during that period was a natural human effort. Traditional norms reflected boys as being more athletic and adventurous. The norm for girls was a desire to learn to cook, sew, and clean house. However, contemporary times convey that boys are predominately athletic, courageous, and macho, but girls too now lean toward athletics and adventure. In light of our physical makeup, women are more delicate than men and were once honored as such. Fifty years ago, women driving forklifts was unheard of; women simply were not hired to do strenuous labor. Only in recent years have we seen female truck drivers, especially, big rig,

OTR (over the road) drivers. We now see women in numerous areas of employment. We have flag ladies in the construction field, building inspectors, police officers, etc. On the other hand, an increased number of males now choose jobs once designed for women. Many males today would rather be secretaries (white-collar worker) than mail carriers (blue-collar worker). In the past thirty years, we see far more male nurses and CNAs (Certified Nurse's Aide) in addition to beauticians and nannies. Some women prefer to be the breadwinner and have the father keep house and raise the children. The dynamics or driving force involving the exchange of roles inevitably relate to our changing society. For quite a while, Women's Lib and new labor laws have taken precedence over traditional norms. As a result, men with traditional values reluctantly lose the battle against female equality in the workplace. If women faced the limitations of yesterday, the poverty rate would increase. The average family simply cannot survive on one paycheck. Yet traditional men find it difficult to deal with the enigma of aggressive, overly ambitious women. Despite the inevitable position of the now-desperate female, many males find the scenario eccentric.

## Men Are Visual and Women Are Emotional

Other clichés attest that men are visual and women are emotional. Women rely on feelings—wired with sensitivity and emotions. However, with time, we learn to think rationally—learning to analyze a situation before judging it. By mere observation, girls are more self-conscious than boys are and are more likely to harbor hurt feelings. Scenario: "Tommy, you sure have large feet!" Primarily, Tommy (twelve years old) may be so accustomed to hearing those words that it is like a joke. As boys sometimes do, he laughs it off as nothing. On the other hand, girls are quick to believe the worst when called offensive names. A young male child may respond in the same manner if emotionally abused over a long period, but might also be as deeply affected. We would at least like to think that teenage boys take offensive teasing and criticism more casually. At least, on an average, middle-school boys appear to handle short-term criticism or name-calling better than their younger counterparts. Girls are different, self-conscious, and sensitive.

Some are also perfectionists. Despite male and female diversity, we experience the same human emotions. Except, females tend to overreact. The way we respond to each other is relative to the saying that "men are visual and women are emotional." How many times have we heard these words? A male often proves to respond based on how a female appears to him—whether sexy or flamboyant. A female often reacts based on how he makes her feel—whether he makes her feel beautiful, confident, or ultimately adored. Our unique diversity increases our appreciation for each other over a period. Certainly, by now, we know how valuable we are to one another, yet different.

## From My Heart to Yours

I watched you develop in the wound, I placed you there.
I am the very breath that you breathe—*I am God Eternal.*

I caused you to live and thrive, despite any odds.
Whosoever your guardians, it was I who provided for you.

Every time you were rejected and misunderstood;
I waited for you to allow me to comfort you.

When you were molested and struggled with the pangs;
I took notice and relented to assist—to reassure you.

Even when you refused to pray and call upon me;
I watched and sent my love by my chosen witnesses.

Sometimes, I spoke to you through a song, or situation—
Alternatives for when you would not hear my word.

A few of your disappointments I allowed for your good.
You were naïve and could not foresee the ominous result.

I am sorry that you were hurt by those you trusted;
Deceived by those you believed would protect you.

I apologize for the misguidance of trusted friends;
I am sorry that you were wounded by close family.

*I am God, your heavenly Father* who made you.
I did not intend for any evil to befall you.

Yet, it was my intention to train and prepare you to stand.
It was my plan to make you a soldier—a spiritual warrior.

There, dry your weary eyes—I've always been here for you.
I will restore you, and rebuild your life in every respect.

Call upon me, and I will help you regain your self-esteem.
If you allow me, I will make you a recipient of my promises.

My Grace is always sufficient for you, because I sent my Son;
He paid your debt in full—all of your sins were erased.

As you receive my healing—I will give you grace to forgive.
You must forgive in order for your transgressions to be clear.

Once you accept my Son; acknowledge Him as your Savior.
Then, declare Him as Lord over your life, you will have peace.

I faithfully and gladly await your cordial reply.
With understanding, love, and compassion, *Eternal God!*

## The Aftermath of Katrina:
### The Irony of a Catastrophe

(September 2005). We weep, we pray, and tune in daily to keep up with the overwhelming disaster of Hurricane Katrina. The sights are phenomenal: water stands as high as ceilings, cars and other debris float amid the murky waters of New Orleans, and victims are diverted to various locations. Some are transported to shelters, residences, and hotels miles away. We watch poignantly while America and the disaster victims lash out to blame our local, state, and federal government—placing upon them all responsibility for the New Orleans evacuation mismanagement. Anchor personnel, government officials, and others join the victims in a blatant effort to show our government its flaws. There seems to have been no apparent evacuation strategies in place. In addition, the arguments suggest that the people of New Orleans were deliberately neglected. On the contrary, Michael Brown (former FEMA [Federal Emergency Management Agency] (director) insisted that there were no federal funds allotted for immediate emergency efforts. In fact, the media reported that victims were days receiving assistance and official evacuation, which was after the storm hit. Before cleanup efforts can began in the Gulf Region, thousands search for their missing loved ones and friends. Our president makes several trips to the disaster zone to reassure its victims of a well-structured and promising recovery. Louisiana governor, Mayor Nagan, and state officials make public declarations of rebuilding the city as millions of funds pour in from across the United States and neighboring countries.

First, most of New Orleans's storm victims are within or below poverty status and had no means by which to divert to safety apart from government assistance. Secondly, government officials (on all levels) have known for some time that New Orleans alone would some day face this magnitude of storm. They also announced that a rated-3 storm would overcome the levies. Thirdly, the City of New Orleans is surrounding by water and stands below sea level. Therefore, the few who evacuated prior to the storm benefited the most. At any rate, we know that we cannot depend on the government alone to follow through on procedures that concern our safety; neither can we expect them to do what we can do for ourselves. It appears that each city, state, and individual community must learn an important lesson from this incident. We all might consider planning our own evacuation and survival strategies—at least an implemented plan for pre-evacuation that may win federal approval. However, we all realize that a storm of the magnitude of Katrina causes for higher intervention. In the mass of outreach efforts, help is coming in from across the country—nearby Jordan, France, Cuba, and other nations. Church representatives, firefighters, police officers, and other organizations from across America have joined our troops in the Gulf Region. The irony of the catastrophe is the compassionate, humanitarian acts of the people. For too long, religion, cultural differences, political parties, and socioeconomic status have separated us. However, all are directly or indirectly affected by this and other disasters. Everyone is compelled to help his neighbor. In our pledge of allegiance to the American flag, we say, "One nation under God . . . ," yet we live as if we are individual nations within a republic rather than states in a union.

"God has always sent His prophets to warn nations of coming judgment or enemy attacks," says Orthodox Christian leaders, "and it is evident that He uses the same method today." We cannot deny the fact that God always sends a warning before disaster strikes. In the book of Amos 3:7, we find that God first reveals his secrets to his prophets. In the third chapter of Amos (Old Testament minor prophet), God also sent warnings to Israel before their enemies overtook them. In retrospect, do we recognize a spiritual connotation to natural disasters and atrocities like 9/11?

Three weeks following Hurricane Katrina, Hurricane Rita surfaced off the Gulf Coast, forcing a massive evacuation of over two million. Even more deadly than the wrath of the hurricanes were the horrendous deaths of twenty-four elderly patient evacuees. All in good faith, Texas officials learned from the Katrina disaster that they must get their people to safety before Hurricane Rita struck land. Unfortunately, a busload of patient evacuees faced an even more gruesome atrocity. Twenty-four patients lost their lives when an explosion caused fire that ripped through their bus. The patients were being transported to safety when the accident occurred, leaving only a few survivors. In addition, others who needed the mandatory evacuation stressed out by the frightening effort to avoid the storm and were more stressed when they faced a gas shortage. In their search for gas, thousands, forced to wait several hours, ran out of gas, or encountered a transportation breakdown. The New Orleans region suffered the worse scenario. Someone stated, "It's like kicking a man when he is already down." Such was the case when Hurricane Rita hit the Gulf

Region three weeks following the Katrina disaster. The ominous aftermath of flooded levies was not something New Orleans residents expected, just to have Rita come along and flood the same areas that had begun to recede.

Listening to the opinions of everyday people prompts one to assess his (or her) own views. First, we listened to facts submitted by emergency specialists, who stated that it is no surprise that a storm of this magnitude would someday hit the Gulf. Next, directors of FEMA stated that they simply were not prepared for this type of emergency. In addition, FEMA representatives publicly complained that their hands were tied during the Katrina disaster. They said that there were far too many channels to go through in order to rush evacuation efforts. Nevertheless, the American public, along with political figures and others, agree that there was simply no excuse for the New Orleans rescue failure. Experts estimated that over ten thousand lives were lost. The scenario is considered one of the most critical acts of negligence in recent history. The public also feels that our government is too quick to run to rescue foreign countries while neglecting their own citizens. Most believe that this incident will lead to more social unrest and greater division. At any rate, it will take the perpetual care of the American public to help in restoring victim's lives. Furthermore, many affected by the storm devastations lean toward reform. Some appeared on TV with Franklyn Graham and voiced their opinions on the need for spiritual revival in the New Orleans region. Contrariwise, others boast of returning to the nightlife of New Orleans culture.

## When Will the Battle End?
### (A Soldier's Aftermath)

Autumn was that season that ushered in a refreshing feeling like spring; a relief from the burning summer heat, I enjoyed the nice cool rain. I sat alone one evening, enjoying a game of sports. I wondered, *Should I watch this game or check out Family Court*. As the game became more interesting, there was a commercial break. I went in the kitchen for a cup of coffee and some cake. In my heart was a surge and sudden ache from a song, which rang in my ear. The message from the song was very loud and clear. My focus shifted as I pondered the words within, so I phoned and shared my conviction with a friend.

In less than forty days, we were on our way, leaving for training camp—me and my friend Ray. Each day brought a new challenge—the experience was appreciated, but some was not exactly what we anticipated. We were fortunate to be together, training only a few days apart in all kinds of weather. We practiced using our chutes, as Ray shouted, "Are you afraid? Are we just two fools thinking we're prepared?" I paused for a moment, then to myself I said, *Am I being brave or am I really afraid?* Finally, I said to Ray, "Man, lets do it. No fooling around; we owe it to our country. I'll see you back on the ground."

Wow! What a jump! So exhilarating, everything went well. Ray was pleased that all was okay just like me I could tell. "Hooray!" we all shouted with glee. "Man, I sure am glad you didn't land in that tree," Ray joked. We couldn't be around him without having our humor provoked.

We wished for Christmas at home during the snow; but war broke out in Kosovo, and we all had to go. I hated the bombing and seeing the innocent killed because in my heart I knew it wasn't God's will. Dear God, I thought, *please don't hold this against us; we are under the captain's command—we must obey and keep focus.*

Ninety days at war with paratroopers jumping, our clothes were soaked and wet, our adrenaline pumping. Days were slow and dreary as things came to a halt; one soldier cried with panic when his foot was caught. "A booby trap," yelled the sergeant as he hastened to the sight; we freed that soldier's foot and asked if he was all right. In much pain and shock, he passed out in our arms; we rushed him for treatment. We kept him safe and warm.

Now, the memory linger from hearing our comrades groan, but worse than that is knowing some still ache and moan. We share a mutual pain deep beneath the skin; it is the ongoing battle that rages from within—feelings of confusion, sadness, and regret, and thoughts that wonder why this war and was it worth the sweat. However, real men must stand up and fight for what is right; no matter what it takes to win, we must uphold our plight.

But when will the battle be over, where do we go from here? How do we abandon the bad thoughts and hold the good ones dear? When will the battle be over? Where does the killing stop? How do we leave this valley and ascend the mountaintop? When will the noises cease from inside our heads? How do we forget the gruesome sights of the wounded and the dead?

Do our families still love us? Does our government care how we represent them and their promise to share in world peace and diplomacy, upholding our constitution? We vowed to assist our troops in bringing a solution to political injustice—one nation against another. We vowed to help keep peace between our allied brothers. But when will it all be over? When will the flags sail free? When will there be unity between you and me?

• Special thanks to Spartanburg Tech for choosing this story (prose) in the Celebrate the Arts competition (2004).

Honors received: Blue Ribbon/ Certificate of Excellence

# Inspirational

## HOME AGAIN

*As a Pilgrim traveler*
*on this restless shore;*
*Sharp arrows pierce*
*my weary soul.*
*Suffering and pain,*
*Grief unexplained;*
*Poignant departure of*
*loved ones untold.*

*In my relentless travel,*
*Amid the mundane;*
*I aspire to know my*
*Master's plan—*
*How he will mold me,*
*Renew, and take me*
*to that promised land*

*At last, Christ-centered,*
*to him surrendered;*
*I gratefully share his*
*glory so grand.*
*Shed tears if you may,*
*He sent angels my way;*
*With Him I am home again*

## IN THE SHADOW OF THE ALMIGHTY
*Psalms 91:1*

*In Christ my savior I hide
The spoiler cannot find me,
Lurking evils cannot molest
Devised weapons cannot harm me,
My foes dare to oppress
I am aimed and at my best
In my Master's serene shadow
Clear of the tempter's arrest
Aware am I, of his foolish games
It is for my soul he aims.
Safe and blessed my Lord doth hide me
His plausible promises sure.
In his presence—beneath the shadow
Of his wings—I am secure.*

## Literary Heaven

*On sound waves from heaven third-gentle voice speaks—*
*entity of king and throne, convey the true belief.*
*Father, Son, and Holy Spirit—by faith alone can I hear it*
*sentient sound as peaceful as sleep.*

*From literary heaven, verse transmitted, trickle*
*soft whispers, shimmering glory untold*
*on my ear—tis on my ear—comfort mind and soul*

*On sound waves from heaven third—angels lift joyful song*
*windsong, heartsong, dewdrops of inspiration*
*precious word pebbles, amid affirmation*
*live within me, amazingly, these tones now seem my own*

*From literary heaven, the great somewhere*
*tranquil verse, consolate relief*
*upon me descend, sentiments within*
*confirm the true belief.*

## Mercy Defies Justice

*Entering the courtroom*

*I sense the threat of revenge*

*Guilty am I, as guilty as sin*

*Justice and prosecutor embrace*

*Each pound upon me with a hard face*

*In an attempt to explain my position*

*The judge says, "Just answer the question!"*

*The footsteps of justice echo deep inside me*

*Suddenly, a light mist fills the courtroom—glorious,*

*This phenomenal scene—coupled with stillness so serene*

*Out of the mist appears an ancient one who calls hastily to the judge*

*Your Honor, I have in my hand a declaration of pardon*

*The judge says, "Sir, who are you? The ancient stands—shoulders wide*

*"I am 'Mercy,' a branch of the Tree of Life."*

# Sovereign!
## (One True God)

*Creator of both heaven and earth*
*Ruler of the universe—the*
*Only God worthy to be served*

*He shines through Christ our Savior*
*His splendid glory we adore*
*Skies display his splendor o'er*
*Mountain, stream, and shore*

*Lets all worship him, ye His people*
*How he awaits our praise each day*
*His presence is all around us*
*And He hears us when we pray*

*Armies can ne'er surround Him*
*There's no entity that can bind Him*
*Mere religion cannot define Him*
*Sovereign, He alone is God!*

## The Bible

*Roadmap through uncertainty*
*Teaches faith and continuity*
*Written by the scribes of old*
*Greatest stories ever told*

*Inspired by the Holy Spirit*
*Entails land saints to inherit.*

*Greatest book of them all*
*Reaches beyond the walls*
*Religion, race, and creed*
*An enlightenment to read*

*The book of hope and trust*
*Introduces Eternal God to us!*

# The Color of Grace

**On** *the level of divinity-the virtue of grace is defined*
**It** *is in the essence of its purpose that the soul is refined*

**G** *is for **green**-significant of life and abundance*
**R** *is for **red**- the blood for me the king did shed*
**A** *is for **ameythst**-royalty that dispels my despondence*
**C** *is for **copper**-His richness in a blend of brown and red*
**E** *is for **emerald**-the gem who suffered in my stead*
*Put them all together, and they spell Grace*
*The priviledge of every tribe, creed, and race*

# The Crisis of a Great Nation

*She once honored the customs of early settlers here;*
*She practiced their beliefs and admired their blissful cheer.*

*She began each day with prayer and devotion*
*Cults now impose by unfair proportion.*

*We cherished chapel where we sang a song of praise;*
*Compared to this era, those were the best of days.*

*How awful the trend of the sexual revolution,*
*Diseases are so intense, for some there is no solution.*

*Censorship, citizenship, and partisanship untold;*
*Now, the world's melting pot, bleak atrocities unfold.*

*Moral decline and injustice—greed has an ugly face;*
*Social and political issues escalate—each demands debate.*

*"America the beautiful," once her proud reputation;*
*Among her traits of decline is renowned acclamation.*

## The Seekers' Prayer

*Make thy servant pure, Oh Lord—my heart, my mind, my soul*
*Anoint me to speak revelations that have only half been told*

*The battle is not mine; it is recorded in your word*
*You are the mighty host of war—my armor, shield, and sword*

*Make thy servant pure, Oh Lord; fill me again with thy spirit*
*Grant me gifts which come by grace, those I could never merit*

*Make thy servant pure, Oh Lord, instead of worldly fame*
*Wash me in thy precious blood—betroth me in thy name*

# Inspirational and Informative

## Am I but a Tree?

*If I could but speak, to say the least,*
*I'd solicit an ear to my saying*
*Inclined to defend, make you comprehend*
*The essence of my staying*

*Of provincial care, my leaves filter the air*
*I produce a world of herbs and food,*
*Besides the comfort of shade, I too upgrade*
*The quality of your neighborhood*

*Notice how you commute o'er smoothly paved*
*Routes—destinations who can compute*
*Another genre of me, the rubber tree*
*Your prized attribute*

*Fuel in winter—green, dry, or splinter*
*The cabin or house where you dwell*
*Try pencil and paper, the sweet taste of maple*
*My uses are many to tell*

*Your fine chest of cedar—porch swing, a three-*
*seater; crossties beneath the rails doth lay*
*an oak desk if you may—the porch swing where*
*you sway; life for you is sweeter*

*Gazebos of oak—a wardrobe for your coat*
*A wooden, gold-trimmed picture frame*
*Without me, what would the world be? I am*
*valuable you see—am I but a tree?*

# From Africa to Riches

*There, there, quiet ye—child of slave molest*
*Daughter of incest; all you've seen is sorrow*
*Lest you cry too long, miss that silver lining*
*Drowning tears deny you that glimpse of light*

*There, there, leave behind those chains*
*Son of slavery—peeled of your dignity*
*Come up from the low place to dawning day*
*Smooth and black your skin, forced to blend*
*midnight to earth tones, shades that never end*

*Hush now, nev're you shed another tear*
*Your ancestors already bear the pangs*
*Shipped ov're the great waters of peril and*
*Brigands—twas them that endured the shame*

*Stolen, your identity—enslaved, your blackness*
*deemed a curse, bring you to low degree*
*Culled in the midst of a cruel world; blind were*
*they to the common bond of humanity*

*Just you take heart now—time is far spent*
*Divine sovereignty makes all things new*
*Let it take you to the plain of dreams—help you*
*embark upon promises long overdue*

*No longer hidden are your abilities; your ingenuity*
*made history. On record your many contributions*
*weary hands that built nations, villages unending*
*Your ethnic heroes through you commended*

## Gotta Climb Atop That Mountain

*It is ever before me*
*Can't seem to avoid its sight*
*Sadly, I descended it*
*when I failed to do the right*


*First, merely a slip, couldn't*
*tell how much the blunder*
*At its foot I wept sorely*
*My fall is yet a wonder*


*Passersby gazed judgingly*
*And jeered as I fell*
*Some even spread falsehood*
*Difficult to prevail*


*Yet, I must climb atop that*
*Mountain—I must*
*Mount a higher plain*
*Gotta drink from that fountain*
*My position maintain*

## Let the Children Show Us

*With strength of youth, clever discerners of truth*
*Minds that are clear, they are eager to hear*
*A dressy jacket with jeans or two-piece name brand*
*Whatever the scene, soon to fulfill their dreams*

*The few that are strong—seek where they belong*
*Learn from their test, try earnestly their best*
*To answer our inquiry—earn their place in history*
*They justify position—resist any opposition*

*Let the children show us!*

*With talent to create, to produce, to invent*
*Each study with the intent and aspire to become:*
*Doctors, lawyers, nurses, preachers, bankers, builders,*
*Tellers, and teachers*

*Witty, reserved, aggressive, or shy—shoulders tall*
*Heads lifted high*
*They blossom, they shine—happiness is theirs to caress*
*Wealth and riches are theirs to possess.*
*They examine, they choose—the future is theirs*
*They have nothing to lose*

*Let the children show us!*

## *Discovering Yourself*

Are you a teacher, homemaker, sports commentator, or a high-spirited entrepreneur? Could you be an inventor? I am sure that George Washington Carver didn't always know what his potentials were. Could Benjamin Franklyn have known his potential of becoming an inventor? Most of us barely discover our abilities early in life. Every now and then, a prophet of God, a family member, or some gifted individual might discern our hidden abilities. But we seldom know who we really are until later in life. Many speak of having dreams of becoming great in some field or another, like Joseph of (Genesis chapters 37–45). Some of his brothers hated him because of his dreams of greatness. However, the dreams came to pass after he was sold into slavery in Egypt. Forewarned of God years in advance, Joseph came to power.

## *My Son Kenneth*

Summer 1985. Kenneth comes into the kitchen. "Mama, I want to play little league football; it is $25 to sign up." I knew that my son and his friends played scrimmage nearly every day whereas they had older neighbors who taught them the basics. Soon the little league season would begin. So at age eleven, I took him to the coaches and paid the fee; soon he was off to becoming a member of the Redskin's little league. Let us face the fact. If there is no incentive to keep a child focused, the possibility of raising an achiever is slim. Children, who have no particular interest sometimes, possess the greatest potential. Many who squander their development period sometimes become late achievers. At the time, football served as a schoolmaster to teach my son (Kenneth) discipline, responsibility, and teamwork. It gave him a sense of belonging and pride. Kenneth and his teammates also learned respect for their elders and peers; they developed a high regard for leadership through their coaches. Having been raised in church also provided a sense of balance.

## Did Kenneth Know He Was a Teacher or Businessman?

In 1989, Kenneth made the football team at Broome High School. Ninth grade at Cowpens Middle School had been difficult for him the first year. He said to me, "Mama, I am not happy there; they don't even have a football team!" From this point forward, it was rough sailing for him. However, as soon as he entered tenth grade at Broome High, the sun began to shine for him again. In 1993, he pulled up his grades, and was awarded best offensive lineman. Of course, I had offered him an incentive. I promised to buy him a car if he pulled up his grades and maintained a good attitude. He followed through, and I bought the car: black Maxima (bar/sunroof/loaded). Before he knew it, he was a senior preparing for the exit exam. Passing the exit exam and meeting college entrance requirements, Kenneth was off to Gardner Webb University. Maryland State had come to "scout" him out; however, Gardner Webb was his choice. In 1999, Kenneth graduated with a BS in management of information systems. Continuing his regimen of studies in business, he also acquired a master's degree in security of information systems in 2004. Often speaking of a drive he could not shake, he took a little time to research the possibility of pursuing a doctorate. I may be a little hypothetical, but I do not think he will stop until he has a doctorate.

## Rosa Parks

Rosa Parks, a prominent profile that graces the halls of history, earned acclaim following her acts of courage and faith. Did she know she would make history? Perhaps she never dreamed of triggering a boycott in Montgomery, Alabama. However, her refusal to give up her bus seat to a white passenger marked the beginning of the civil rights movement in the South. This historical 1955 event marked the end of segregation on Montgomery city buses. A seemingly small act of courage won Mrs. Parks the honor of *"Mother of the Modern Civil Rights Movement"* as well as other accolades. In the course of her upbringing she perhaps, never dreamed of becoming such a renowned honoree. Many people reading this probably have never discovered their potentials, and perhaps, feel that they are just ordinary people. However, everyday those same people tend to make the greatest contributions to society: in inventions, discoveries, creations, and ideas. Discover who you really are, it might surprise you.

His third year at Gardner Webb, Kenneth's yearbook profile read, "Ken Dawkins: 5 ft., 9in., 235 pounds., fullback, Cowpens, South Carolina. Has been one of the more promising players for the Runnin' Bulldogs over the past two seasons. Had possibly the best spring practice of any player on the roster. Will be a prime candidate to start in the offensive backfield. Excellent hands for a back. Finished the season with thirty carries for 112 yards. Was team's leading ground gainer. High School: Played at Broome High School (Spartanburg,South Carolina--played linebacker and offensive tackle.

## Life Is like a Ball Game

*Game of life, four bases:*
*Sovereign Creator, you, purpose, and goal*

*We enter and endeavor to know our places*
*Divine purpose to take control*

*First base: We don't know what to do*
*Instead, we rely on God to see us through*

*Second base: struggle, too many goals to*
*Juggle; so we submit to him our trouble*
*Although we foul and miss the mark*
*He knocks the ball clean out of the park*

*Third base: priorities together*
*Finally focused regardless or whether*
*Learning to regroup at midlife*
*We take things more in stride*
*Tranquil when cumbering subsides*

*Home base: Just when we would*
*give up, God gracefully shows up*
*All-season coach by our side*

# Silent Cry of a Victim

Ere, the shadows of blackness bombard my soul,
I am but a child—my life invaded by this grim and bitter cold.

Many risings and settings of the sun ushered me here;
a place where I too soon awake in fear.

To see the blackness ravish my mother, molest my father,
and peel away the color of beauty—away from them and us;

My sister and my brother
Dread the grim shadow with disgust.

Ghastly, it creeps upon our senses—we've hardly a chance to resist.
Distorted, their understanding, fooled are they by a subtle twist.

We cringe when they beat them, bow when they cry "nigger,"
I look ahead to the day I leave, the time I'm bigger.

Can't let that grim shadow follow my life;
Gotta seek who will help me abolish this strife.

I hate talking down to them—I feel what they feel;
to be slaves was not their choice, neither is it my will.

## Street Moods

*City smog as condense as smoke*
*rush hour traffic is no joke*
*Neighbors shout "Hi," from*
*a nearby roof*

*Skateboarders challenge one*
*Another—each looks out for the other*
*Heed sound of horse's hoofs*

*Shoppers walking, businessmen talking*
*Transits line Fifth Avenue*
*Subway cars gliding*
*pause for those riding*
*Compelled to move on through*

*On balcony, wind chimes*
*Clanging beneath is gangbanging*
*Joggers choose Central Park*
*At stop light, commuters pacing*
*Pondering tasks they are facing*
*start for home, and it is now dark*

# Sunshine after the Rain

*Where there is no vapor, there is no cloud*
*If there is no cloud, there is no rain*
*Where there is no rain, there is no change*
*There can be no sunshine after the rain*

*Where there is toil, there is pain*
*If there is pain, faith serves to sustain*
*Where faith sustains, there is gain*
*There is greater faith after the pain*

*Where faith increases, there is change*
*If there is change, faith remains*
*Where faith remains, there is gain*
*There is sunshine after the rain*

## Tragedy at Columbine High

*The day moves along as usual*
*there is no threat in sight*
*When suddenly gunfire surrounds*
*us, and our day turns into night*
*There are continuous explosions*
*you can nearly cut fear with a*
*knife—all because of someone's*
*anger, bitterness, and strife*

*While some are blasted to their*
*deaths, others manage to hide*
*Mr. Sanders does his best*
*to lead some of us outside;*
*when he too is shot in an heroic*
*effort of love. Quietly, he slips*
*away and enters his home above.*

*Along with twelve students*
*who did not survive—Mr. Sanders*
*will always be in our hearts,*
*and with us ever abide.*

# Wisdom

*She comes from afar to accompany knowledge
on his mission
Small voice of discretion, always proficient,
always precise*

*She articulately coaches each recipient of
her ingenuity
Condescends in service unto the least
of intelligence
Glides like an eagle along the steeps and
valleys of the mind
Warrants each endeavor—assures each
protégé his plight*

*She transcends to guide the prophet,
the skilled surgeon, the king, and the poet
To the prophet she gives foresight,
To the skilled surgeon, she gives prudence,
she is the kings advisor,
And to the poet she gives understanding.*

*She is captain of the ship of exploration,
Commander of the ship of endeavor,
Pilot of the ship of accomplishment;
She is navigator of the ship of destiny.*

# Longing for the Night

*Poor, poor me, a mother of three*
*You ask me what my take would be*

*If I could be free from strain and toil*
*The demand of clean, bake, and boil*

*I would seize the night—so serene*
*Relief from bake, boil, and clean*

*The silence of night takes me away*
*Rest mind and body like a mt. stay*

*Serenade of birds, song of the brook*
*No demands to clean, wash, nor cook*

*I'd stretch myself out on a chaise*
*The sweet serene, warmly embrace*

*Reach for my mind—wondering*
*Gather up my heart's—pondering*

*Ov'r dreams dormant, nev're end*
*Think of family, confidant, and friend*

*Stressed is me—mother of three*
*Declaring what my take would be*

*To be free from bake, boil, and clean*
*Seize the night—so serene*

## Laretha Sinclair Furgason

### The Mysterious Lady

In March 1985. The weather is cold and sunny, but she's walking. Upon entering the market, she doesn't seem as rushed as before. Often shopping here, I felt I'd see her again. Feeling she's someone special, I anxiously wish for the moment we meet. And today I get my wish as she walks toward me on the cereal aisle. I reach for the cereal, and she says, "Hello, what is your name?" Somewhat nervous, I reply, "I'm Laretha Sinclair Furgason, who are you?" She smiles and says, "Just call me Rita." Somehow I don't believe that's her real name, but I smile pleasingly. We both freeze up and turn to leave the cereal aisle. I notice that she has features like the Furgasons; I also think she's interracial. There has to be some explanation for the way I feel. Something about her radiates making me feel warm inside. Next, I find my foster parents (Aunt Ida and Uncle R. L. Furgason), and we grab a few more items just before going to the checkout. Surprisingly, she appears at the next register and glances longingly. Mama looks a bit surprised and waves as if she knows her. The look in their eyes says more than mere words. All evening I'm wondering what Mama knows. On the way home, I ask her and Papa if they have seen Rita before. They seem to ignore me and instead choose to discuss rising prices. Finally, Mama says, "I've seen the lady a few times." Entering the long driveway, Papa says, "Let's get the groceries in so we can look after the horses before it's too late, kitten." I can see he's evidently doing his best to deter my thoughts, so I go along with him. Besides, I look forward to seeing the horses. The "Diva" is my horse; she's a beauty with a cold black tail and mane and has black around her ankles like Dana (her dad). She gallops gracefully. Riding her makes me feel I am soaring; I forget my worries. Then there is the foal that belongs to the palapino mare; it is fun to watch. At least assisting Papa gives me a chance to ride the Diva. A half hour passes before we complete our duties at the barn. I ride the Diva, and we head home. Walking at a slow pace, Papa is singing one of his favorite hymns. It is too complicated for me to accompany, so I just listen.

### Spring

It is the first Sunday of spring, and Mama is a little late returning from worship. She assists with communion and helps to tidy up afterward. Papa is especially careful to let her know I am leaving with him, and then we head for home. Mama says that is why she drives on first Sunday, so it is not necessary for us to wait for her. Papa drives slowly as if meditating. Soon we reach the driveway, and the dogs come to greet us.

On the inside, we go to our rooms to get comfortable. In thirty minutes, Mama is driving up the driveway, just as I finish changing my clothes. At least she won't have to remind me this time. Rushing in the door, she says, "Gosh, it's somewhat chilly out there." Papa has coffee brewing, and the aroma fills the air.

Before too long, Mama is in her apron. Papa hands her a cup of Maxwell House to warm her up. Before too long, with Papa's assistance and mine, dinner is on the table. Having filled all the glasses with ice, I pour the tea and anxiously take my seat by the bay window where I sit to watch the horses. Diva (my horse) is a little over three years old. I love watching her prancing along with the foal. Immediately following dinner, there is an interesting phone call. Mama is talking with someone who asks how it is raising a girl at her age. Next, I hear her speaking softly, saying, "We run into her at the market sometimes. She seems okay." I wonder if she's speaking of Rita, Could she be talking to someone who knows her? In two weeks, Becca (Furgason's daughter) will be home on spring break. I will ask if she knows who Rita is. We have grown close, and if she knows anything, she will tell me. Besides, everybody's making plans for their scholars to return home on spring break, and Mama and Papa prepare for Becca's arrival. Soon a week passes, and she calls to confirm the date. I ask when she is supposed to arrive. Mama answers, "April 10." Reaching for the calendar, she confirms that it is the following Friday. It is all I can do to keep from asking about the lady at the market again, but I must wait until Becca is in and ask her.

## The Dream

One afternoon, I fall asleep on the den sofa, then I find I am dreaming. The dream takes me to a different time and place. There is a border of snowy pines and a snow-covered walk with beautiful evergreen shrubs on each side, barely seen beneath the snow. The walk leads to a quaint (old-fashioned), two-story brick house. There are also columns, smoke ascending the chimney, and an old Lincoln in the driveway. It seems that I live there with parents who are upset with me about something. There is a tall young man sitting by an open fire holding a baby. His

countenance portrays worry and anxiety. Then the dream ends.

## The prayer cathedral

A short ways from where we live, there is an old cathedral. I never see children go there alone, but I must go. I must talk with someone about Rita, about how I long to know my dad, and about the answers to my dreams. One Saturday afternoon, I ask Mama if I can go for a walk. Answering, she says, "Don't be too long, Retha. Dinner will be served at five o'clock." Dashing out the door, I rush into the street toward the cathedral. On my way there, I ponder over my questions. Upon reaching the steps, I brace myself and try to calm down. As I enter the center aisle, there are a few people kneeling. Most unusual for this time of day, I thought. However, I take a seat while waiting for someone to speak with me. As other seekers enter the center aisle, one of the mothers enters from a side door. When she comes up the side aisle, I quickly reach out to her. Gently she asks, "Can I help you, child?" Rising from the pew, I reply, "Yes, ma'am!" She then motions for me to follow her into a long hallway where we walk through double doors. Taking my hand, she leads me to a small room where we sit for several minutes. Beginning with a prayer, she makes sure that I am not a runaway or homeless, then asks my name and reason for coming to the cathedral. She tells me she is known as Mother St. Elizabeth. On the wall of the room is a clock with chimes,

so I watch it constantly to make sure I do not stay too late. Pausing, I inform her that I am to be home by five o'clock. Rising from her seat, she reaches for me and holds me by the shoulders, saying, "Everything will be all right." We then turn to leave the room. As she walk me down the long hallway, I sense a strange peace about her.

## Rebecca Arrives

On Friday, April 10, we hear a horn, and somebody yells, "Hello, everybody!" Papa then dashes through the side door with a shout, "Hello there! How's my baby?" Rebecca swings around his neck as I wave from the patio. He then grabs one of her luggage and head for the steps. Mama runs out to meet her as I wait for my turn. When they start up the steps, I reach for her, and she nearly sweeps me off my feet. Holding my hands, Becca gently pushes me away from her and says, "Gee, you've grown. How's my little sister doing?" I grin with excitement. As soon as we get her all nestled in, she looks over the house and brags on how well it is kept. Taking some of the credit, I smile with a deep sense of pride. We all stay up later than usual and go up for bed around midnight. Becca and I spend a lot of time together on Saturday, but most of the late evening she spends with Mama. So Papa and I watch a movie until we become too sleepy to stay focused. On the way to my room, I hear Becca and Mama talking, speaking with someone on the phone. Eavesdropping, I hear Becca saying, "Hello, Rita, how have you been? Yes, she's grown a lots. Well . . . And how long will you be in town?" Going to my room, guilt grips my heart like fear, but I can't believe what I've heard. They do know Rita. Restless, I toss and turn an hour before falling to sleep. Sometime or another, I sense someone kissing me good night. I suppose it is Becca. However, just before daybreak, I slip into a deep sleep and dream that Rita comes over; the dream is short and vivid. The next day, Becca asks me to brisk-walk with her. We start our regimen and later stop to rest. Comfortable with her, I ask if she knows Rita and share how I sense some mysterious connection with her. Becca asks my loyalty and makes me promise to never breathe a word; she then explains that this is not a good place to talk. So she lays out a plan. "Let's go home and take a shower, then we'll go out for lunch and talk at the park." About an hour later, we take the freeway. Safely weaving through traffic, we reach the park by 2:20 p.m. Looking at me, Becca says, "Retha, you must never let Mama know that you know anything." Sipping on lemonade every now and then, she begins, "You see, Mama's brother (Uncle Walter McArther) is Rita's father. He left for the marines when she was only thirteen years old. They say he found another love and married, rearing two boys from that union. Ned Sinclair (your father) was stationed in Hawaii, so Rita returned to Virginia to care for her mother. With both a sick child and mother, she was overwhelmed." Becca looks at me with tender compassion and continues, "Retha, honey, you were born premature and had some health problems. Ned and Rita— young and immature—made plans to place you in a special home by the time you were four. But Mama and Papa took the initiative to ask for you; she always wanted another child anyway. Eight weeks later, we went to pick you up at Rita's family home here in Virginia. By this time, you were showing very little signs of premature syndrome. Ned was sent overseas, Rita cared for her mother, and we brought you home with us. It was like my little sister coming home. Besides, when we visited, I would hold you in my arms and dream of you living with us. Rita is really Uncle Walter's daughter, but he never married her mother. He is your grandfather. And yes, Rita is your biological mother. Her mother died within six months after we brought you home, so she went to be with Ned and spent time with her father on occasions. But she always checked on you while in town and promised to never interfere. Everyone felt it was best you not know Rita and Ned are your parents until you are older. Uncle Walter agreed; he feels that Mama and Papa's love brought you through. They all felt it was good for you and I to have each other. Look at you now; it seems you were never premature. I love you, Retha. You are my sister and cousin!" With tears streaming down both of our faces, we embrace a few moments and head for home. On our way home, we said very little and there was a pleasant quietness in the atmosphere. The kind of unusual peace I feel when I am with Mother St. Elizabeth.

### More Dreams

Soon after Becca's conversation and mine, I have a recurring dream. This time, there seems to be one or two changes in the dream. I am caring for someone who is ill, the young man is no longer present, and the baby is in a hospital. Everything seems like a puzzle. Then the dream ends. The day Becca returns to college is fast approaching. She and Mama have washed and packed all of her clothes. Before, she left me feeling abandoned, but now I feel as if someone has taken her place.

My relationship with Mother St. Elizabeth is just what I needed. Her blessings put my mind at ease. The day finally arrives when Becca leaves. After our good-byes, I go off to my room to try to absorb many of the things she shared with me. Drama, she calls it. I feel better now that she has answered some of my pressing questions. I knew there was something about Rita, but I could not figure it out. Soon I will talk with Mother St. Elizabeth about my dad (Ned Sinclair). I must find out where he is and how I can see him.

After Becca returns to college, I spend time at the library with Yunna, but I visit the cathedral alone. When Becca calls, I share my visits to the cathedral. She encourages me to be strong and heed the council of the Christian mother. Somehow I feel I am being prepared for some serious surprises, as Mother St. Elizabeth said.

### Dream of a Man in Sports Vehicle

It is midsummer, on a Monday evening. The air conditioner is on, so I fall asleep on the den sofa. Dreaming, I am walking with Yunna near the city library on a fall afternoon. Suddenly, we notice a tall stranger reaching for his car door. He waves with a stare. Comfortably dressed and neatly combed, he gets into a sports car and drives off. The sweat suit he is wearing reminds me of one Papa wears. The dream then takes us to where Yunna lives (one block above me) across the street. Yunna and I lounge on a lawn chair as we notice the same car moving slowly toward us. This time, he seems as if he is looking for some place in particular. His tag reads, Seattle, Washington. Then the dream ends. I awake with a new anxiety, wondering if the man in the dream is my dad. Just as I felt about Rita, I know there is also something special about this man. Something must have happened to my dad since no one has seen him in a long time. Besides, why does he come to mind now? After deeply pondering over the dream, I go into the kitchen for a snack. Papa teases at me, and I pause to give him a hug. He and Mama are wonderful to me. Mama has been upstairs mending a few items but stops to come down and join us. Stepping through the café doors, she says, "What are you two munching on?" Papa chuckles, "Mostly anything we can get our hands on, sweetheart." To my surprise, Mama says, "Do you know that it has been seven years since we've seen Ned?" All of a sudden, the pictures she moved from the living room, and the man in the dream all come to mind. Continuing, she adds, "I'll see if anyone has heard from him lately. I heard he's back in the States." They haven't a clue that I know who Ned is. Tuesday can't come fast enough for me. As soon as breakfast is over, I am going to see Mother St. Elizabeth. However, it is instead on Tuesday afternoon that I tell Papa I am going for a walk. He looks at me and says, "Don't be too late. Your Mama wants you home for dinner!" Off I go as fast as I can. All that is on my mind is seeing the holy mother. Reaching the site, I pound upon the cathedral walkway and into the sanctuary with great anticipation.

Inside, I take a seat by the east aisle. If Mother St. Elizabeth is counseling today, it won't be long before she comes out to take a look around. Nearly fifteen minutes pass before she appears. In sole desperation, I fasten my eyes upon her and we connect. She seems to feel what I feel and motions for me to come to her. Walking through the hallway, she shows me the water fountain where I take a drink. We then enter the conference room where we met before. The quaint setting with the huge antique clock reminds me of something I saw in a magazine. Soon the chimes ring out four o'clock, and then she begins the blessing. Afterward, she listens to my dreams and pauses to read a passage from Proverbs 15:22. The passage reads, "Without counsel purposes are disappointed; but in the multitude of counselors they are established!" Somewhat puzzled, I ask what the saying means. Then, she takes my hands in hers and says, "Retha, we all have a purpose here, but we don't always know what it is. And when we need guidance, God answers in His own way." I start to ask her to listen to my last dream, but she just repeats the same saying, "Retha, when we need guidance, God comes to us in mysterious ways. Your dreams carry a message, soon you will see." The chimes ring out five o'clock, so she reminds me to go home right away. Embracing me, she smiles with confidence. She then escorts me down the long hallway and through the aisles of the sanctuary until I exit the front doors. This time I feel my faith grow. I know I'll see my biological father again and get to know Rita and granddad, Walter McArther.

## Labor Day Weekend

Becca phones to say she is bringing a friend to meet the family, and Aunt Nell and Uncle Blake writes to say they are bringing Mama Rose (Mama's mother) to the cookout. At eighty-seven years old, she moves along quite well, or so Mama says. We are all very excited about everyone coming. Tomorrow, I will invite Yunna and her cousins from Sudan, Emman, and Manassah. When we met, I could tell right away that they don't mind that I am interracial. I'm glad we live in a diverse community. Papa is African American, and Mama is interracial. Maybe that's why my African friends feel okay with me. Papa teaches Sunday school, and I heard him say that we are all one in

Christ, if we are born again. In September 1985, Uncle Blake, Aunt Nell, and Nanna (grandmother) arrive at eight o'clock sharp. Papa and I help them into the house while Mama sets the table. As everyone greets the other, emotions run high. After all, it has been a year since we've seen each other. We all laugh as Mama kisses Nanna from cheek to cheek.

She is most pleased with the way they have cared for her, saying, "Mother, you look great, considering all you've been through!" Uncle Blake speaks up and says,

"This girl has a strong will. She's a fighter." Now washed up for breakfast, we all sit for the blessing. Aunt Nell carries on over how I've grown. I share that I'll be thirteen in a few days and will celebrate my birthday. Time passes as we wait for Becca and her friend to arrive. In anticipation, Yunna, Emmun, Manassah (my African friends), and I spend some time together. They are eager to teach me French, and we share family history—what little I know. It is exciting watching them play kickball. Emmun and Manassah are also good at basketball; they are on the high school team.

## Rebecca Introduces Her Future Husband

On Labor Day morning, Becca and her friend Noal arrive at 7:15. Anxious to meet him, we rush out to assist with the bags. Noal is every bit what Becca says he is—tall, medium-built, and good-looking. "You must be Retha," he says, smiling at me. "Yes," I reply. Since it is the first time we meet, he gently shakes my hand and pats me on the shoulder. Now that I've met Noal, Becca and I must talk. I must tell her about the intense conversation Mama and Aunt Nell had last night. Around nine o'clock, I join Becca for a long walk, to inform her of the tension between Mama and Aunt Nell. Papa, Uncle Blake, and Noal spend time with the horses and walk the old grape orchard, which gives Becca and I quality time alone. To my surprise, she tells me that we have other family coming to the cookout, someone I may not remember. Two hours before dinner, Mama calls us all into the den to prepare us for the unexpected surprise. Turning to me, she says, "Retha, there are relatives coming to join us today that you havn't seen in a long time." Nanna then takes the floor, "Retha, try to be strong, baby. Your life will come together today." Becca puts her arm around me and says, "It will be all right, honey." Just before our mysterious guests arrive, Aunt Nell and Papa take me aside to explain the surprise. However, I continue clinging to Becca. Judging from Noal's attitude, he already knows what is going on. He loves Becca, and they are close. I am sure that they share everything.

## Retha Meets Her Family

Waiting for Rita, Ned, and granddad McArther to arrive—my mind goes back to a time when I am younger. After seven years, it is like a light bulb going off inside my head. I recall pictures of my family. Now, I know why Mama put them away. She was afraid I would long for them if I saw their pictures everyday.

Yet I do see Rita from time to time, although she does not look much like she did in the pictures. Besides, I was only four years old at the time. Soon, a two-tone SUV drives up at the curb, and who steps out but Rita. Next, Ned—resembling the man in my dream—steps out on the driver's side, and Granddad McArther gets out of the backseat. Everyone runs out to greet them as I watch from the walkway. I notice Aunt Nell embracing Rita and Ned as if they are her children and speaks as if she is very close to them. Mama interrupts the greetings by asking everyone to come inside for a short meeting. Papa and Uncle Blake fire up the grill while we talk. Upon entering the downstairs parlor, Mama asks if I recognize Ned. I stare at him and recall the dream, which is more recent than the pictures she put away. Pausing, I ask him if he is my dad. He nods his head and reaches for me. However, my attention goes to Rita. She looks at me with guilt and love and says, "I have always wanted to tell you, but I promised not to interfere." They both walk over and put their arms around me, and we shed tears together. Bonding through our tears, we continue to stand there until Ned suggests that we all sit. With Rita on my left and Ned on my right, it all comes into play: the dreams, my feelings about Rita, and the pictures disappearing. Everyone is teary-eyed except Nanna. Mama says she is strong and wise. Speaking, she says, "Ned and Rita, it's all over now. Retha knows everything, and you can take her and give her what she really needs. Ida and Richard are retired now. They need to spend this time enjoying what they have left. I know they will never admit it, but I can see that they don't feel up to raising a girl as young as Retha. Sure, they love her, but she needs to be with you now. You all need each other." Mama weeps sorrowfully as if I am leaving today but doesn't say anything. Becca can't take any more of the drama, so she goes out to assist with the cookout. Ned pulls me closer to him as Rita keeps her arm around me. It takes us forty-five minutes to get through this poignant moment. Exiting the parlor, Nanna then says, "Thank God, it is over—no more secrets." Suddenly, Papa comes in and insists that we all come outside and get something to eat. Granddad McArther pulls me to his side and says, "You are with your family today, baby. Enjoy the moment. I have waited a long time for this day, but I kept up with you, pumpkin." Out on the lawn, Nanna puts her arms around me and adds, "Try and understand, darling. Your parents were both young and didn't know what to do back then. Give them a chance, and they will make you very happy. I've talked with them about you." I reply that I believe God had been preparing me for this day. My friends walk up and join us. Taking a moment, I introduce them to my family.

*To be continued . . .*

## What the United States Flag Means to Me
### By Cephus Javon Thompson III

What the United States flag symbolizes is spelled out in its stars, stripes, and colors. The United States flag represents power, blood, and the fifty states. The power means that we are wealthier than some other countries through our faith in God, military, and intelligence. Our flag is also a symbol of unity, loyalty, and victory. The United States flag also represents blood. The red stripes represent the blood that veterans, soldiers, and patriots shed for our country. The last thing the United States flag symbolizes is its stars that represent the fifty states. The states they represent are the following: Alaska, Arizona, California, Nevada, New Mexico, Utah, Colorado, Washington, Montana, Wyoming, Oregon, Texas, North Dakota, South Dakota, Louisiana, Minnesota, Iowa, Nebraska, Oklahoma, Arkansas, Missouri, Kansas, South Carolina, Alabama, Wisconsin, Illinois, Indiana, Kentucky, Tennessee, Georgia, Florida, North Carolina, Philadelphia, Ohio, New York, West Virginia, Delaware, New Jersey, Pennsylvania, Connecticut, Massachusetts, Vermont, New Hampshire, Michigan, Idaho, Rhode Island, Hawaii, Maine, Maryland, Virginia, and Mississippi. Although each individual state has a different flag, the flag of the United States was designed to represent all states as a union. That is why they are called the United States of America.

# Introduction to Children's Book
## Mr. C the Riverbank Beaver

Once upon a time, an old grey beaver built his lodge high on the riverbank. Many beavers lived nearby, but Mr. C lived high on the east side of the river. As the oldest of his kind, he went along his way quietly.

Everyday, the young beavers played near Mr. C's burrow, laughing and bouncing from branch to branch and rock to rock.

On a warm sunny morning, Mr. C's neighbor, Ms. Seemore, was hunting food for a tasty breakfast. She said, "Good morning, Mr. C." Slowly and lazily, Mr. C answered, "How do you do, Ms. Seemore?" With a great big smile, she replied happily, "Very well, thank you!"

When Mr. C noticed that Ms. Seemore did not find any food, he offered her some buds. To his surprise, she accepted, saying, "Thank you very kindly, Mr. C!"

The young beavers had always wondered why Mr. C had such an odd name, so they mustered up the courage to ask him about it. Young Gerald asked, "How do you do, Mr. C?" Turning to see who spoke to him, Mr. C replied, "Hello there, young fellow!"

Gerald poised himself and said, "Mr. C, may I ask you a question?" In a deep, cloudy tone, Mr. C answered curiously, "What can I do for you, young Gerald?" Gerald asked, "Why do they call you Mr. C?" Amazingly, Mr. C asked Gerald to sit down. He then proceeded to answer him, saying, "You see, when I was young like you, I was clumsy and dropped nearly eveything I picked up. So my Papa called me 'clumsy' from that day forward. By the time I was five years old, I told everybody my name was C because I did not like being called clumsy."

Young Gerald walked away sadly remembering how he and his friends had often seen Mr. C drop things as well. Together they tried to figure out how to make him not feel so bad about his clumsiness. Soon they talked Mr. C into playing catch ball. To their surprise, Mr. C never missed a ball. All of the young beavers shouted with joy and sang, "He's a jolly good fellow." They lifted Mr. C high off the ground and marched around the forest in glad admiration. Ms. Seemore came out of her lodge to see what all of the commotion was about; other beavers peeked curiously. They tore from their burrows, staring anxiously at the young beavers as they continued the parade. Upon discovering what prompted such a to-do, they joined the party— circling back and forth with makings of the largest country picnic the river beavers had ever witnessed. At last, Mr. C felt a sense of acceptance, and he lived his final years like a prince.

Printed in the United States
By Bookmasters